Tasty Treats

Easy Cooking for Children

Written by Adina Chitu
Illustrated by Elenia Beretta

LITTLE
GESTALTEN

Let's Get Cooking!

You probably know a couple of the dishes that are in this book already and there are probably some you have never tried before. They might become your new favorite treat! First, choose a recipe. Then, before you start, ask a grown-up if they're happy for you to prepare the dish alone or if you ought to have some help—you need to work with sharp knives and hot temperatures with care. Every recipe in this book comes with a list of the ingredients and tools you'll need. Get everything together before you start, so you don't lose time searching for something while you're cooking. Put on an apron and make sure you wash your hands. Now you're good to go! Have fun and— most importantly—enjoy!

Kitchen Essentials

You can create many different recipes with just a few basic utensils. Have a look through the things you have at home and check with an adult which ones are safe for you to use by yourself and the ones you'll need help with. Here are your best friends in the kitchen...

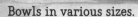

Bowls in various sizes.

Measuring cups in different sizes for dry ingredients such as flour and sugar.

A chopping board for cutting up fruit and vegetables.

1. A sieve.
2. A big wooden spoon.
3. A pastry brush for spreading butter and glazes on food.
4. A knife, which should be sharp, as a blunt one is more dangerous when you're working with food.
5. A grater for shredding hard cheese or veggies such as carrots and zucchini.
6. A rolling pin to help flatten out your dough.
7. A frying pan for cooking up sweet and savory treats.
8. Two different types of spatula.
9. A hand whisk can be used for dry and wet ingredients.

Jars can be used for storing ingredients and spices. You can also use them to carry treats to your picnics.

A blender chops all types of nuts and veggies. You can also use it when you're making smoothies.

Scales, to measure precise quantities of each ingredient—especially important when it comes to desserts.

A hand mixer is super-easy to use and it makes batter smooth in seconds.

A baking sheet for large batches of cookies or for when you're making pizza.

Parchment paper helps to prevent food from sticking to the baking sheet.

Important Ingredients

There are some basic ingredients you should always have at home, but going to a grocery store or a farmers' market on the weekend can be a lot of fun, as there are usually lots of new foods to discover. Just pick the items you think look the most interesting! Here are some of the things you'll need for the recipes in this book, as well as a few handy tips for the best way to store food at home.

Eggs are used in all kinds of sweet and savory dishes.

Leave a banana or an apple right next to an avocado if you want the avocado to ripen more quickly.

Putting an apple in your bag of potatoes helps the potatoes stay fresh for longer.

You'll need vegetables in all colors and shapes. They're full of vitamins and give you the energy you need to play and have fun.

Make sure your fruit bowl is filled with tasty things—pineapples, apples, pears, or bananas.

If you turn your pineapple upside down, the juice from the bottom will be distributed through the entire fruit.

Olive oil is good for your skin! You'll need it for dressings and frying.

Flour and sugar are needed for many sweet recipes.

There are different kinds of both—try some out and see how different your food tastes.

Salt and pepper bring every dish to life. Most of the time you just need a pinch of each, and then the magic happens!

Put your sprigs of herbs, such as parsley, basil, or dill, in a glass of water and store them in the refrigerator. This will keep them going for longer.

7

Pancakes with Fruit

There are many ways to cook pancakes. Here is a basic recipe that you can use with different toppings. Pancakes are often eaten as a special treat for Sunday breakfast and they're usually served stacked up into a small tower—the tallest yet was created in the U.K. and was more than three feet (one meter) high!

You will need:

- 1 large bowl
- 1 hand whisk
- 1 frying pan
- 1 big spoon
- 1 spatula

Ingredients:

1 egg

150 g flour
(¾ cup)

1 tablespoon sugar

1 teaspoon baking powder

1 teaspoon vegetable oil

Fresh fruit, plus hazelnut spread, maple syrup, or jam, to serve

200 ml milk
(¾ cup, plus
2 tablespoons)

1 Combine the milk and egg in the bowl and whisk by hand until the egg has dissolved in the milk.

As soon as tiny bubbles appear on the pancakes' surface, you can flip them using a spatula. Once they've turned a brownish color on both sides, you know they're done!

2 Add the flour, sugar, and baking powder to the bowl and whisk again until you have a smooth batter.

3 With the help of an adult, place the frying pan over a medium heat and pour in the oil. Once it's hot, pour a spoonful of the batter into the pan—see if you can fit three pancakes in there at the same time!

8

4 Stack a couple of them up on a plate so that you have a tower, then add your favorite toppings.

Add jam or hazelnut spread between the pancakes and create a cake!

Juicy Fruit Salad

There are so many kinds of fruits. They come in lots of different shapes and colors—and flavors, too. Happily, they don't just taste good, they are also extremely healthy. You can combine your favorite fruits to make a delicious salad, and you can change the ingredients depending on the season and what is available when you're making it. Here, we show you how you can even skip the bowl and eat your lovely salad out of a melon instead. Make sure you wash your fruit first!

Ingredients:

- 1 kiwi, peeled and sliced in half
- 1 peach, sliced in half and de-stoned
- 6 strawberries, tops removed and hulled
- 1 small melon
- 10 blueberries
- The juice of ½ an orange
- 2 teaspoons maple syrup
- 1 tablespoon almond flakes

You will need:

- 1 knife and chopping board
- 1 tablespoon
- 1 citrus squeezer (optional, as you can squeeze the orange by hand if necessary)
- 1 medium bowl (for the dressing)

1 Slice the kiwi, peach, and strawberries into big chunks.

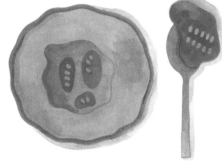

2 With the help of an adult, cut the melon in half, scoop out the seeds using the spoon, and hollow the pulp out of both halves, so they can become your salad bowls. Put the pulp and juice to one side.

3 Arrange the fruit chunks, the melon pulp, and the blueberries in the melon halves.

4 Now make a "dressing": mix two tablespoons of the melon juice with the orange juice and maple syrup.

10

To test if a melon is ripe, knock on its "shell". If you hear a dull thump, it's ready to be eaten.

5 Pour the dressing over the fruit salad and sprinkle the almond flakes on top. You can either serve them straightaway or keep in the refrigerator for a few hours.

Guess Who Toast

Grocery stores have a huge selection of products on sale, but have you ever considered making something yourself from scratch? This is a lot of fun! Here is a healthy version of an all-time favorite, hazelnut cream with crunchy nuts—and it comes with funny faces.

Ingredients:

· 200 g chocolate, broken up into pieces (1 cup and 1 tablespoon)
· 100 g walnuts (1 cup)
· ½ an avocado
· 4 slices of toast
· Fruit, such as banana, blueberries, or strawberries
· Oat flakes, almonds, or additional walnuts

You will need:

· 1 large saucepan
· 1 small saucepan or bowl that can rest inside the large saucepan without touching the bottom
· A blender, or a plastic bag and a rolling pin
· 1 bowl
· 1 fork
· 1 big spoon
· 1 knife and chopping board

1 You will need to ask an adult to help you with this. Fill a saucepan one-third full with water and place it over a medium heat. When it starts to boil, place the chocolate pieces in the smaller pan, or bowl, and place it over the larger one. Watch out that no water bubbles into the chocolate. Stir until it melts, then turn off the heat and put the bowl to one side.

2 Crush the walnuts using the blender or put them in a plastic bag and smash them into tiny pieces using a rolling pin.

3 Mash the avocado with a fork in the bowl, then add the melted chocolate and crushed walnuts. Then mix it all with the spoon until you get a smooth spread.

12

4 Everything is ready to serve now, so start decorating
the slices of toast with faces of your favorite animals!

Cover the toast with
your chocolate spread ...

... use oat flakes for
feathers ...

... banana slices for
eyes ...

... an almond for its
nose ...

... give its eyes
blueberry pupils ...

... and add slices of
strawberries for wings!

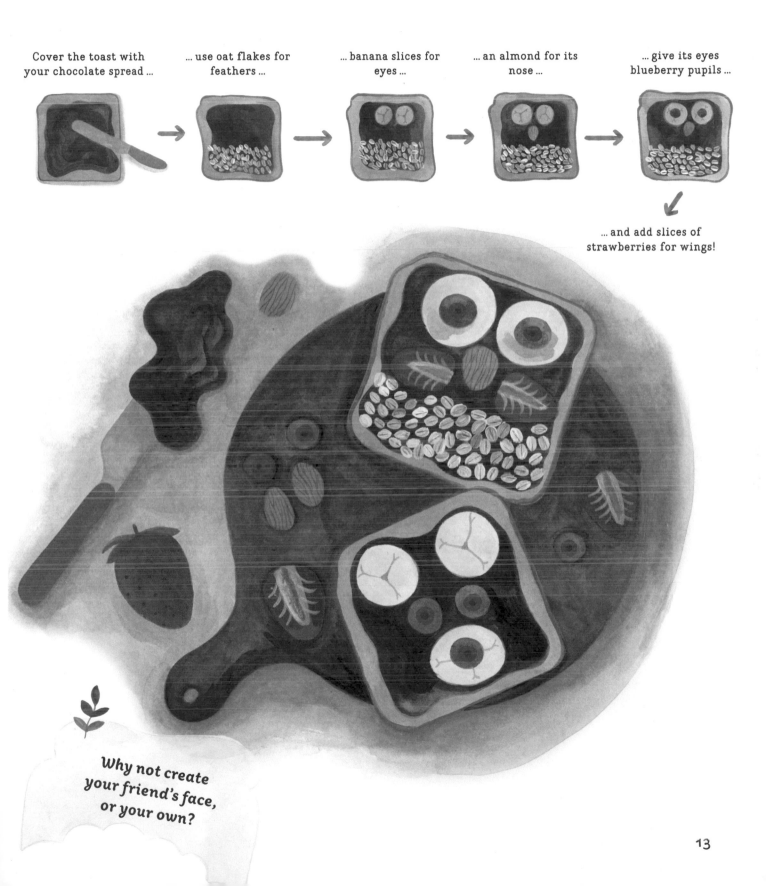

Why not create
your friend's face,
or your own?

French Toast

French toast is loved all over the world, which means it's got lots of different names—eggy bread, German toast, and poor knights, to name just a few. It's not only really easy to make but also a great way to use up any bread that needs eating up. Sweet versions are usually served with maple syrup or jam. Some people like them as a savory treat and add ham.

You will need:

· 1 large bowl
· 1 hand whisk
· 1 plate
· 1 frying pan
· 1 spatula
  (for flipping
  the bread)

Ingredients:

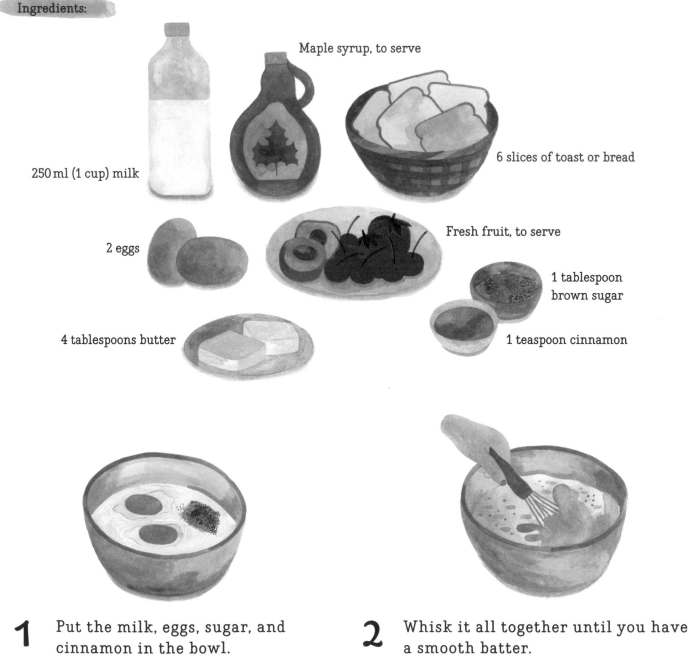

250 ml (1 cup) milk

Maple syrup, to serve

6 slices of toast or bread

2 eggs

Fresh fruit, to serve

1 tablespoon brown sugar

1 teaspoon cinnamon

4 tablespoons butter

1 Put the milk, eggs, sugar, and cinnamon in the bowl.

2 Whisk it all together until you have a smooth batter.

14

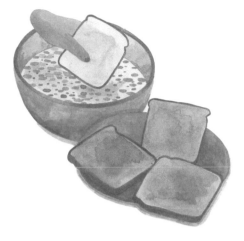

3 Dip each slice of bread in the batter for a few seconds, then set to one side on the plate.

4 With an adult helping you, melt two tablespoons of the butter in the frying pan over a medium heat, then add as many slices of bread as you can and fry both sides until they are slightly brown. Fry the remaining slices, adding the rest of the butter as necessary.

5 Serve warm with fresh fruit and maple syrup drizzled over the top.

Add two tablespoons of flour to the remaining batter and make some crepes in the same pan!

Egg Sandwich

Sandwiches are a popular classic that can be prepared in many different ways. Here, we've added a twist to the top layer to make it the perfect snack—and you can fill it with the things you like most.

You will need:

· 1 cookie cutter
  or drinking glass
· 1 frying pan with lid
· 1 spatula

Ingredients:

· 2 slices of toast
· 1 tablespoon
  vegetable oil
· 1 egg
· 1 knob of butter
· 1 slice of ham
· 1 slice of cheese
  (such as Gouda)
· 4 slices of cucumber
· 2 slices of tomato

1 Use the cookie cutter or glass to cut out a shape or hole in the middle of one of the slices of toast.

2 With the help of an adult, add the oil to the pan, then add the toast with the cut-out, and, over a low heat, fry it on one side for two minutes.

3 Flip it, crack the egg, and pour it carefully into the hole.

4 Put the lid on and fry it for a few more minutes, until the egg is cooked. Then, fry the second slice of toast on both sides.

5 Spread the butter on the second slice of toast.

6 Top this with the ham, cheese, and salad veggies.

7 Place the slice of toast with the egg in on top, then serve. If you cut it in half, you can see all the different layers and it's easier to eat!

If you want a vegetarian version, just leave out the ham.

17

Rainbow Salad

Vegetables are so versatile, tasty, and tempting. It's hard to resist the smell of a fresh tomato, the sweetness of a crunchy carrot, or the refreshing hit of biting into a cucumber baton. But we have to admit, vegetables are even tastier when they look fun, and this salad comes in a rainbow of hues. We recommend preparing it in a jar with a lid so you can take it with you to school or a picnic. Actually, you better take two of them—your friends will all want to try your creation!

Ingredients:

· 2 small carrots
· 2 small cucumbers
· 1 red pepper
· 1 small can of chickpeas
· 1 small can of sweet corn
· 3 tablespoons olive oil
· 1 teaspoon mustard
· 1 teaspoon honey
· 2 teaspoons lemon juice
· A pinch of salt and pepper

You will need:

· 1 knife and chopping board
· 1 sieve
· 3 bowls
· 1 large spoon
· 1 jar with lid
· 1 hand whisk (or fork)

1 Using the knife and chopping board, thinly slice your carrots and cucumbers into discs, then slice the pepper first into strips and then into small rectangles.

2 Open the can of chickpeas and, using the sieve, drain the contents and rinse them with fresh water, then place them in one of the bowls. Repeat with the can of sweet corn.

3 Use the spoon to add the vegetables to your jar to create the layers of your rainbow: first add the chickpeas, then the carrot, cucumber, pepper, and finally the corn.

4 Now, on to the dressing! Here are all the ingredients you need.

5 Put the olive oil, mustard, honey, lemon juice, salt, and pepper in the third bowl and mix using the hand whisk. Pour the dressing over the jar's contents and you're good to go!

You can also use any other vegetables you have at home. Create a rainbow in your favorite colors!

Lemonade

During hot summer days, lemonade is a super-refreshing drink. It's easy to make and, once poured into a clean bottle with a lid, it's easy to take along to a picnic and share with friends. Classic lemonade only needs lemon juice, sugar, and water, but you can add other fruit if you like, or herbs such as rosemary—or even vegetables like cucumber.

You will need:

· 1 knife and chopping board
· 2 bowls
· 1 big spoon
· 1 measuring jug
· 1 hand whisk
· 1 sieve
· A jar or carafe (at least 1 liter)
· 1 citrus squeezer (optional, as you can squeeze the lemon by hand if necessary)

Ingredients:

10 strawberries

3 teaspoons honey

A handful of fresh mint leaves

2 cm fresh ginger

1 lemon

1 With an adult helping you, peel and thinly slice the ginger.

2 Place the ginger in one of the bowls, add the mint and honey, then stir.

3 Boil 500 ml water (2 cups), pour it over the ginger and honey mixture, combine it using the whisk, then leave to rest for 30 minutes.

4 Using the sieve, pour the infused water into the other bowl, separating it from the ginger and mint.

5 Slice the strawberries, then thinly slice half of the lemon.

6 Add the fruit slices to your jar or carafe, then pour in the infused water.

7 Squeeze the other half of the lemon over the top, then add another 500 ml cold water.

8 Stir with the spoon, then put the lemonade in the refrigerator for a few hours. If you can't wait, serve it with ice.

You can try mixing the flavors up. If you love watermelon, add a big slice of that instead of the strawberries!

Picnic Time!

Hot summer days should be celebrated with a picnic, whether you're headed to a park, the lake, or even just your backyard. There are lots of tasty treats in this book that you could pack up and take with you—here are a few ideas for how you can spend your day in the sun.

So that you're as comfortable as possible, pack some blankets and cushions. Practical things to remember are sunscreen, hats, and maybe some mosquito repellent.

You probably won't spend the whole afternoon eating. With just a few props that are easy to find in nature, there are a couple of games you can play with your friends. Hide-and-seek is a popular classic, and you could also build an obstacle course using stones and branches you're likely to find nearby.

Savory treats you can prepare ahead of time are the cheese crackers, quesadillas, and some rainbow salad jars. Yum!

If you've got a sweet tooth, make sure you take some muffins and chocolate balls. How about some pancakes, too?!

Drinks like lemonade can be transported in glass bottles with lids.

23

Spooky Muffins

These muffins get dressed up as ghosts and might scare some people, but they are actually very sweet on the inside. Make sure you get an adult to help you with this recipe.

For the frosting:

· 250 g mascarpone cheese, at room temperature (1 cup and 1 tablespoon)
· 50 g butter, at room temperature (¼ cup)
· 1 tablespoon powdered sugar

You will need:

· 3 large bowls
· 1 hand mixer
· 1 spatula
· 1 muffin tin and 12 paper muffin cases
· 1 large spoon
· 1 knife

Ingredients:

· 250 g flour (2 cups)
· 1 teaspoon baking soda
· 1 teaspoon baking powder
· 1 teaspoon cinnamon
· 100 g butter, at room temperature (½ cup)
· 150 g sugar (¾ cup)
· 2 eggs
· 150 g Greek yogurt or sour cream (¾ cup)
· 2 tablespoons milk
· 150 g raspberries, fresh or frozen (1 cup and 2 tablespoons)
· Blueberries, to decorate

1 Mix the dry ingredients in one of the bowls: the flour, baking soda, baking powder, and cinnamon. Set aside.

2 In another bowl, mix together the butter and sugar using the hand mixer, until you have a smooth dough.

3 Add the eggs, one at a time, mixing again after each.

4 Add the yogurt (or sour cream) and milk and mix once more, then add the flour mixture and combine using the spatula until you have a smooth dough.

5 Add the raspberries to the dough and gently fold them in. Heat the oven to 200°C (fan) / 390°F.

6 Place the muffin cases in the tin and, using the spoon, fill them equally with the dough. Bake for five minutes, then turn the oven down to 180°C (fan) / 350°F and continue cooking for 15 minutes.

7 Using the third bowl and the hand mixer (paddles cleaned!), make the frosting by mixing its ingredients together until smooth.

Ghostly goings-on

Turn it upside down!

8 Remove the muffins from the oven and let them cool completely. Now it's time to dress them as ghosts: Slice the tops off some of them, take these out of their cases and turn them upside down. Smother them all with the frosting and use the berries for eyes.

Flowerpot Dessert

Imagine the surprised faces when you tell everyone that there's a tasty dessert hidden in these flowerpots! This layered cake—which needs no baking—is very simple to prepare and makes a fun decoration for the table before it's time to tuck into it. Everyone can get a personalized pudding—just use different herbs and flowers.

Ingredients:

- 10 chilled Oreo biscuits (or any dark cocoa-based biscuits)
- 10 strawberries, tops removed and hulled
- 250 g cream cheese, at room temperature (1 cup plus 2 tablespoons)
- 2 tablespoons honey
- Herbs and edible flowers, such as rosemary, basil, thyme, or chamomile, to decorate

You will need:

- A blender, or a plastic bag and a rolling pin
- 1 knife and chopping board
- 1 bowl
- 1 big spoon
- 2 plant pots, ramekins, or small cups
- 1 toothpick

1 With the help of an adult, put the biscuits in a blender and blend until you have fine crumbs (or smash them up using a bag and rolling pin).

2 Cut the strawberries into small pieces.

3 In the bowl, combine the cream cheese with the honey using the big spoon.

4 Now, arrange everything in your pot. First, put a layer of biscuits, then a layer of cream, followed by a layer of strawberries. Repeat once, or twice if you have enough—the last layer should be crumbs, since this is the "soil" of the pot!

26

5 Wash the herbs and flowers, then, using the toothpick, make a hole in the soil and plant them.

Worried about how to keep the rest of the Oreos in the box fresh once you've opened it? Just put a slice of bread in with them—they will stay crunchy for longer.

Easy Ice Cream

Takes 15 minutes, serves 4

On a hot summer's day, there's nothing better than some ice cream melting on your tongue. This recipe is a quick (if you're using frozen fruit) and healthy version that you can vary with any fruit you like!

You will need:

· A blender
· Small bowls

Ingredients:

160 ml yogurt (½ cup)

1–2 tablespoons maple syrup

170 g (¾ cup) mixed berries, such as raspberries, blackberries, and blueberries, fresh or frozen

3 bananas

Ice-cream cones (optional)

1 If you're using fresh berries, put them together with the bananas in the freezer the night before you want to make this.

2 Put the fruit in the blender, then add the yogurt and maple syrup.

3 Blend everything until you get a smooth cream.

Try experimenting with other dairy products, such as quark or cream cheese.

4 Serve immediately in ice-cream cones or small bowls. You can also keep the rest in your freezer for later.

Simple Spaghetti

Making your own pasta sauce at home is really simple. You can store any leftovers and use them later for a pizza (see our version, p. 42). Also, with this recipe, you only need to use one pot when you're cooking!

You will need:

· 1 small blender
· 1 large saucepan
· 1 colander or strainer
· 1 tablespoon
· 1 knife and chopping board

Ingredients:

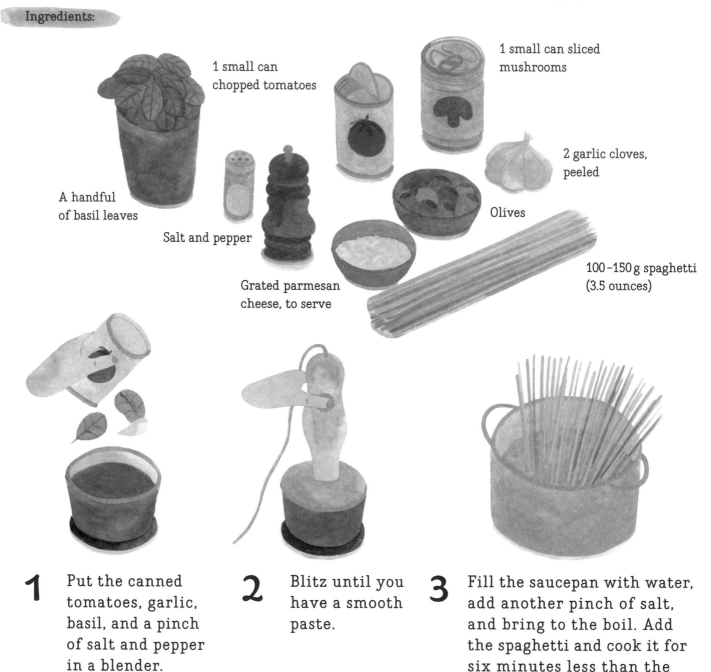

1 small can chopped tomatoes

1 small can sliced mushrooms

A handful of basil leaves

Salt and pepper

2 garlic cloves, peeled

Olives

Grated parmesan cheese, to serve

100–150 g spaghetti (3.5 ounces)

1 Put the canned tomatoes, garlic, basil, and a pinch of salt and pepper in a blender.

2 Blitz until you have a smooth paste.

3 Fill the saucepan with water, add another pinch of salt, and bring to the boil. Add the spaghetti and cook it for six minutes less than the instructions on its packaging.

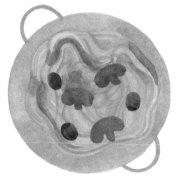

4 With the help of an adult, drain it using the colander.

5 Put the pasta back in the pan and add three to four tablespoons of the tomato sauce. Stir and cook for two to three minutes over a medium heat.

6 Strain the can of mushrooms and slice the olives. Add both to the pan and cook for another two to three minutes.

Put the rest of the sauce in a jar and keep it in the refrigerator—it will last for a few days!

7 Serve with some parmesan cheese sprinkled on top.

Veggie Quesadillas

Quesadillas are a Mexican dish that is the perfect combination of everything your body needs. We've made ours with vegetables but you can put meat in if you like—anything works in these! If you're cooking for friends who aren't keen on veggies, these are ideal for hiding them out of sight!

You will need:

· 1 grater
· 1 knife and chopping board
· 1 frying pan with lid
· 1 spatula

Ingredients:

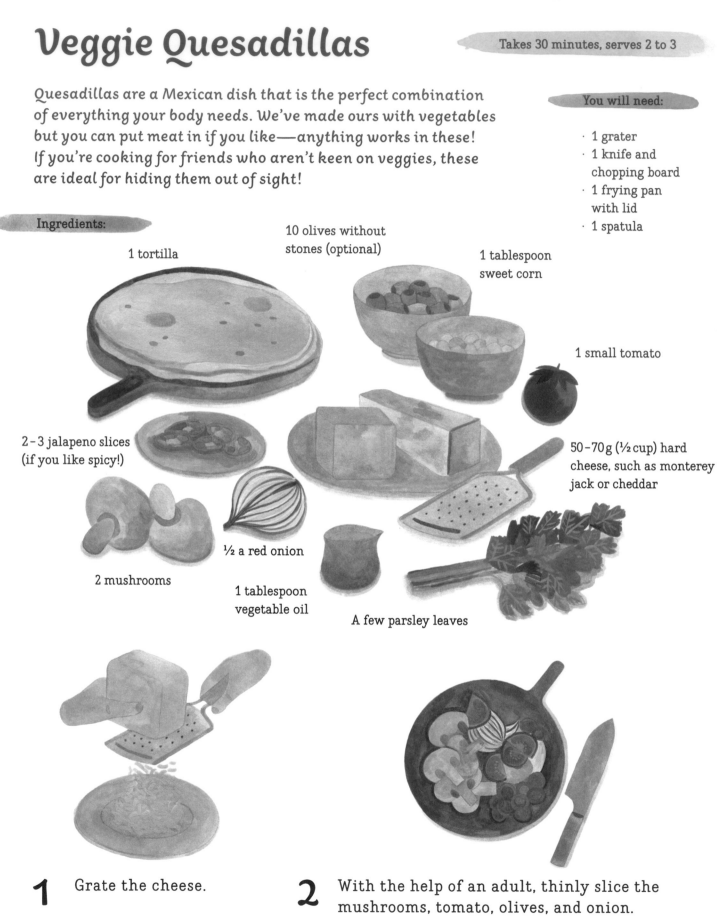

1 tortilla

10 olives without stones (optional)

1 tablespoon sweet corn

1 small tomato

2–3 jalapeno slices (if you like spicy!)

50–70g (½ cup) hard cheese, such as monterey jack or cheddar

2 mushrooms

½ a red onion

1 tablespoon vegetable oil

A few parsley leaves

1 Grate the cheese.

2 With the help of an adult, thinly slice the mushrooms, tomato, olives, and onion.

3 Still working together, add the vegetable oil to the frying pan and place over a medium heat. Add the tortilla to the pan.

4 Turn down the heat and scatter the cheese on top.

5 Scatter the veggies and the parsley leaves on top of the cheese and continue to cook over a low heat for three to four minutes.

6 Using the spatula, carefully fold half of the tortilla over the other half and press down a little. Put the lid on the pan and let it cook for another two to three minutes, until the cheese has melted.

7 Remove from the pan and cut the tortilla into three pieces. Serve with dips, such as sour cream, spicy salsa, or guacamole (an avocado cream).

This is a great dish for using up leftovers.

Chocolate Balls

Imagine chocolate balls as small bites of energy. You can eat these delicious balls as a dessert or snack during the day and, best of all, you don't need an oven to make them!

You will need:

· 1 large bowl
· 1 spatula

Ingredients:

50 g chocolate chips
(¼ cup)

4 tablespoons shredded
coconut, to decorate
(optional)

1 teaspoon
cocoa powder

7–8 tablespoons
honey or maple
syrup

2 teaspoons
peanut butter

2 tablespoons finely
crushed almonds
or almond flour

½ teaspoon
cinnamon

10 tablespoons
oat flakes

If you like dried fruit, you can chop some up and add the pieces to the mix!

1 Combine all the ingredients (except the coconut) in the bowl, mixing them with the spatula, until everything blends together smoothly.

34

2 Make your hands damp, then take small amounts of the mixture and form little balls by rolling them between your palms.

3 If you like, roll some of them in the shredded coconut, then place them in the refrigerator for at least 30 minutes before eating. You can keep them there for two to three days.

Cheese Crackers

Have you ever thought about baking savory cookies instead of sweet ones? These crackers are a truly addictive snack, which is fine as they are pretty healthy. Cut them into different shapes—squares, triangles, and rectangles—and share them with your friends.

You will need:

· 1 grater
· 2 large and 1 small bowls
· 1 hand mixer
· 1 knife and chopping board
· 1 spatula
· 1 rolling pin
· 2 baking sheets
· 1 teaspoon
· 1 pastry brush

Ingredients:

350 g flour (2 ⅘ cups)

100 g sour cream (½ cup)

2 sprigs of rosemary

Sesame seeds, to sprinkle

2 eggs

A pinch of salt

100 g butter, at room temperature (½ cup)

250 g feta cheese (1 ⅔ cups)

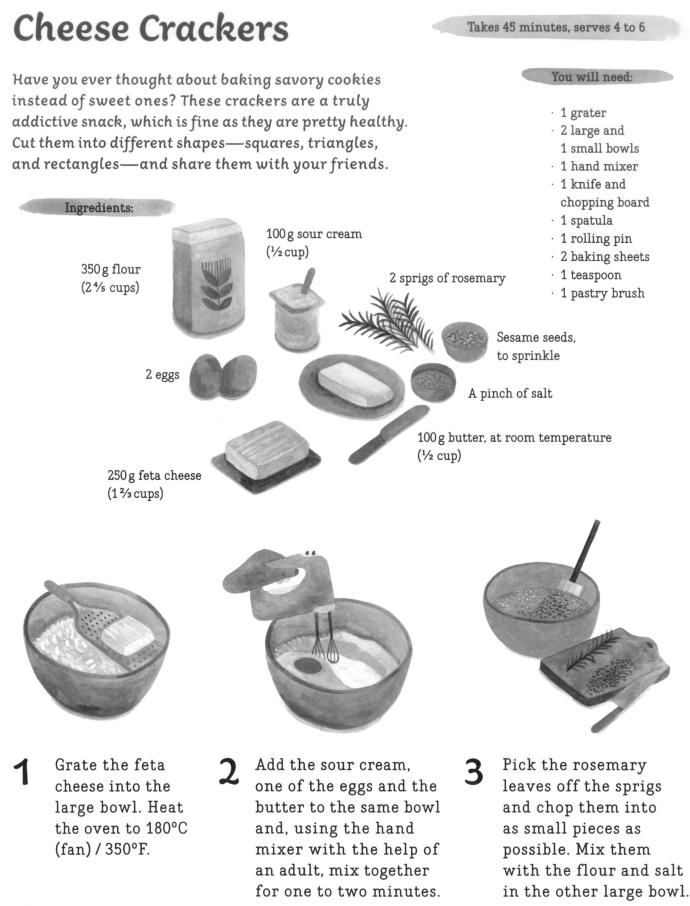

1 Grate the feta cheese into the large bowl. Heat the oven to 180°C (fan) / 350°F.

2 Add the sour cream, one of the eggs and the butter to the same bowl and, using the hand mixer with the help of an adult, mix together for one to two minutes.

3 Pick the rosemary leaves off the sprigs and chop them into as small pieces as possible. Mix them with the flour and salt in the other large bowl.

4 Bit by bit, add the flour mixture to the cheese mixture, stirring with the spatula each time you do, until you get a thick dough.

5 Knead the dough for a couple of minutes.

6 Separate the dough into two big balls, then roll each out until you have a thick layer, then move them onto the baking sheets.

7 Using the knife again, cut the dough into different shapes and make some space between them.

8 In the small bowl, mix the other egg with a teaspoon of water and brush the dough shapes with it. Sprinkle the sesame seeds over the top and place both sheets in the oven for about 20 minutes, or until the crackers are golden brown.

You can serve your crackers with dips, such as cream cheese, salsa, or hummus.

Berry Mocktail

A what? Well, a mocktail is a cocktail without any alcohol in it. If you would like to have a fancy drink, a mocktail is just the thing. Get dressed up and let the dinner party begin!

You will need:

· 1 tall jar
· 1 pestle
· 1 small sieve
· 1 drinking glass
· 1 large spoon
· 1 toothpick

Ingredients:

· 2 sprigs of rosemary
· 5 raspberries, plus extra
· 10 blueberries, plus extra
· 1 teaspoon honey
· Juice of ½ a lemon
· Sparkling water
· Ice cubes

1 Pick the leaves off one of the rosemary sprigs and put these, along with the raspberries and blueberries, in the tall jar, then add the honey.

2 Mash everything with the pestle until the juices come out, add the lemon juice, then stir.

3 Using the sieve, strain the juices from the fruit into your drinking glass, pressing them through with the back of the spoon.

4 Add some sparkling water and ice cubes.

5 To decorate the glass, thread some berries along the toothpick.

6 Garnish the glass with the other rosemary sprig and the berry stick. Cheers!

The Big Feast

What about throwing a party for your best friends and cooking some of your favorite recipes for them?! You could have a theme for your party: It could be a specific color, such as blue, and everyone is asked to wear something in that color. Or it could be to celebrate a special event such as Halloween. Or why not ask them to dress up as the characters from your favorite TV show? Plan a whole afternoon and evening together and don't forget to tell your guests to come hungry!

To get everyone excited, send out invitations to your party with the theme of your party on.

Create a "photo booth" by hanging a blanket on a wall for you and your guests to stand in front of and put out some props. They could be crazy glasses, fun masks, hats, or wigs—anything you can think of. Print the photographs off afterwards and make a gallery of the best ones!

Find out everyone's favorite songs and prepare a playlist that will have your guests rushing to the dance floor. Just ask them what music they like when they reply to your invitation!

You can decorate the food table with tablecloths and plants (or flowerpot desserts) and put paper garlands and balloons up around the room—anything that helps make it look like a special occasion.

Garden Pizza

Cheese Crackers

Flowerpot Desserts

Berry Mocktails

Garden Pizza

Takes 90 minutes, makes 2 pizzas

Making pizza dough at home is easier than you think, because you actually only need a few basic ingredients. This recipe is special, as you use your pizza base as a canvas to create a picture—this one is of some pretty flowers. Share a slice with a friend or eat a whole one yourself!

You will need:

· 1 large bowl
· 1 large spoon
· 1 knife and chopping board
· 2 baking sheets
· Parchment paper

For the pizza dough:

· 300 g all-purpose flour, plus extra (2 ⅖ cups)
· 200 ml tepid water (⅘ cup)
· 2 tablespoons olive oil
· A pinch of salt
· 7 g dry yeast (2 ¼ teaspoons)

For the sauce and toppings:

· A few mushrooms
· A few cherry tomatoes
· 1 pepper
· 1 zucchini
· A few olives
· 3–4 tablespoons tomato sauce (or the pasta sauce from p. 30)
· Small mozzarella balls
· Chorizo or pepperoni slices
· Fresh herbs, such as basil, thyme, or parsley

1 Put all the ingredients for the pizza dough in the bowl and mix them with the spoon until you get a sticky dough.

2 Put the dough on a floured surface and knead it for about 10 minutes, until it gets smooth and elastic.

3 Split the dough in half and let the balls rest on the counter for an hour. Then heat the oven to 230°C (fan) / 450°F.

4 Slice your veggies, so you can use them to create your garden.

5 Cover your baking sheets with parchment paper, shape each ball of dough directly onto your sheets and stretch them carefully until you get a round shape.

6 Spoon some tomato sauce on top and spread it over the dough with the back of the spoon, then add the mozzarella, the sliced veggies, and the chorizo. Get creative and arrange them so they look like flowers or anything else that comes to mind!

The mozzarella balls are fluffy clouds.

The herbs can be grass and the veggies and chorizo can be the flowers.

7 Bake for 15 to 20 minutes. Add the herbs once the pizza is done.

Fried Rice

Fried rice is a popular part of Eastern and Southeast Asian cuisines. As a homemade dish, it's typically made with ingredients left over from other meals, which means there are countless variations.

You will need:

· 1 knife and chopping board
· 1 big frying pan or a wok
· 1 spatula
· 1 plate

Ingredients:

· 2 medium carrots
· 2 spring onions
· 3 tablespoons butter
· 2 eggs
· 2 tablespoons frozen green peas
· One medium bowl of leftover rice, or you can boil some rice and let it cool completely
· 2 tablespoons soy sauce

1 Chop the carrots into small cubes and slice the spring onions.

2 With an adult helping you, place the pan over a medium heat, add a tablespoon of the butter, and let it melt. Add the eggs and scramble them until they are fully cooked, then put them to one side on the plate.

44

3 Let the rest of the butter melt in the same pan. Add the carrots, spring onions, and peas. Cook for five to six minutes, stirring occasionally, until the vegetables are a bit softer.

4 Add the rice and eggs and mix everything together with the spatula. Cook for two to three minutes, add the soy sauce and cook for another two minutes. Then it's ready to serve!

Campfire Bread

Get ready for a true classic: campfire bread. Prepare the dough at home and take it on a trip where adults are going to be making a campfire, or cook it in your backyard over a barbecue. The crunchy bread tastes of adventure in the wild.

Takes 1 ½ hours, serves 6

You will need:

· 1 large bowl
· 1 big spoon
· 1 clean tea towel
· 6 wooden
  sticks / skewers

Ingredients:

300 g all-purpose flour
(2 ⅕ cups)

200 ml tepid water
(⅘ cup)

7 g dried yeast
(2 ¼ teaspoons)

30 ml olive oil
(4 tablespoons)

1 teaspoon salt

1 Put all the ingredients in the bowl and mix them using the spoon until well combined.

2 Knead the dough for about five minutes.

3 Cover the bowl with the tea towel and let the dough rise for about an hour in a warm place. It doubles in size!

4 Shape the dough into six balls and let them rest for a couple of minutes. If you're taking them on a trip, place them in a container with a lid, making sure they're not touching, if possible.

5 Take the sticks and sanitize them for a few minutes in the fire.

6 One by one, take the balls of dough and shape them into ropes. Swirl them around the sticks like they're snakes.

7 Bake them above the fire or heated coals, making sure you keep the dough right above the heat. Turn the sticks constantly and keep checking that the dough isn't burning. Once the bread is golden brown, they're done!

ADINA CHITU
is a food photographer and food stylist based in Bucharest. Her
blog *Pancake Planet* illustrates her passion for food, which started
at the end of 2016 when she left her job in PR and began on this
new journey.

ELENIA BERETTA
is an Italian illustrator living in Berlin and working for clients
such as *Vogue*, *The New York Times*, and *Elle*. She illustrates
cookbooks and children's books. She also loves traveling, cooking,
and skateboarding.

Tasty Treats
Easy Cooking for Children

Written by Adina Chitu
Illustrated by Elenia Beretta

This book was conceived, edited, and designed by gestalten.

Edited by Maria-Elisabeth Niebius and Robert Klanten

Recipes by Adina Chitu

Design and layout by Constanze Hein, Book Book
Typefaces: Quister by Nadia Knechtle, Aisha by Titus Nemeth

Printed by Grafisches Centrum Cuno GmbH & Co. KG, Calbe
Made in Germany

Published by Little Gestalten, Berlin, 2020
ISBN 978-3-89955-148-8

For more information, and to order books, please visit
www.little.gestalten.com.

Bibliographic information published by the
Deutsche Nationalbibliothek.

The Deutsche Nationalbibliothek lists this publication in the
Deutsche Nationalbibliografie; detailed bibliographic data are
available online at www.dnb.de.

This book was printed on paper certified according to the
standards of the FSC®.